Write Now!

The right way to write a story

Karleen Bradford

Cover by Willem Hart
Illustrations by Adriana Taddeo

SCHOLASTIC INC.
New York Toronto London Auckland Sydney

ISBN 0-590-43116-1

12 11 10 9 8 7 6 5 4 3 2 1   9/8 0 1 2 3 4/9

Printed in the U.S.A.   01

First Scholastic printing, September 1989

Contents

Believe it or not,
it's *not* all that hard

1

"Write a short story. For next Monday."

Write a short story? For next Monday? You've got to be kidding!

Unfortunately your teacher is not. So how do you do it?

Believe it or not, it's *not* all that hard...

* * *

The first thing you need, of course, is an idea. Search your mind. Right. It's as blank as that blank piece of paper sitting in front of you. So sit back, close your eyes, and *don't* look at the paper. Think. What's been happening in your life lately? I can hear your answer.

"NOTHING!"

That's not true, though. You're alive, aren't you? Then things are happening. Did the dog chew up your mother's brand-new Italian leather purse? Did you have to babysit a rotten kid? Did you have a fight with your best friend? Did your teacher ask you to write a short story?

Things *are* happening. They don't have to be big, monumental, colossal things. Most short stories start from very small beginnings.

Still stuck? Try brainstorming. It works. Pick up your pencil or pen and start jotting things down. You'll have to open your eyes for this, I'm afraid, and tackle that blank piece of paper, but don't bother about making sense. That's not important right now. Just write down any and every idea that crosses your mind.

For example:
- I've chewed my pencil so hard it looks like a mouse has been at it.

2

- I just heard an enormous noise in the kitchen.
- The doorbell just rang.

And so on and so on and so on. You think they don't sound like ideas for stories? Wait and see what we can do with them.

Another way to generate ideas is to put your mind to work while you're sleeping. Just because *you're* resting doesn't mean *it* has to.

I was asked to write a short story for a school reader once when I was in the middle of writing a novel and didn't really want to take the time off to write a story. It's very flattering when editors ask you for things, however, so I thought it wouldn't be too bright of me to refuse. Trouble was, I couldn't think of a thing to write about.

What had I been doing lately? Sitting at my typewriter every day writing a book. Interesting for me, perhaps, but for somebody else? Boring!

Then I started thinking. I had also just bought a golden retriever pup, and my thirteen-year-old son was taking her to obedience classes.

Still boring. How many dog-and-boy stories have been written? Must be in the millions. I gave up for the moment, but when I went to bed that night I lay in the dark for a while before going to sleep, just thinking about it.

While I was lying there, I remembered a dog that I'd seen while walking my pup one morning. It had lost a leg in a trap, but it could jump fences, play and get around just as well as any four-legged dog I'd ever seen. Maybe there would be something in that.

I told my mind sternly to work on it during the night, then went to sleep. Sure enough, when I woke up the next morning, the beginnings of a story were there to greet me.

What if a boy was determined that his beautiful new dog, descended from a long line of champions, was going to be a champion, too? And then what if *his* dog lost a leg in a trap? Magic words, those:

4

particularly like the image that conjures up. (Might make a good idea for a story, though. What if someone *did* kill two birds with one stone . . . ?)

Take a problem,
stir well

2

Now let's take some of those ideas and play around with them a little.

- The dog chewing up your mother's purse, for example. What did your mom think about that? What did the cat think about it?
- What about babysitting the rotten kid? What did she do? What did you do?
- Fighting with your best friend? What was it all about? How did you feel? How did your best friend feel? What if it was all over a misunderstanding, but neither of you knew that?
- Your teacher asked you to write a short story? What if the school fell

down — would you still have to hand in that story?

• While chewing your pencil you accidentally swallow the eraser and start to choke to death and there's nobody else home. (I know, I know. That's a bit far-fetched, but we're just fooling around here.)

• There's an enormous noise in the kitchen but (again) you are alone in the house and you *know* there shouldn't be anyone in there. Did you remember to lock the back door when you came home?

• The doorbell just rang. It's either that friend you were fighting with, or your mom, who forgot her keys and is about to find her purse all chewed up, or . . . or . . . or . . .

So far these have just been aimless ramblings, but by now something will have struck a spark. There's a glimmer of interest there somewhere. Pounce on it. You've got a problem of some kind? Make it worse! A story has to have a plot, and that's what this is all about. What happened? What happened next? And then what happened after that? How does it all turn out? Choose one of your ideas and take it further.

- Your mom didn't want the dog in the first place. She likes cats instead. She's bound to make you get rid of it now. (The cat, by the way, is looking very smug.)
- After you finish cleaning up the mess that rotten kid made, you suddenly realize you haven't been keeping an eye on her — and now she's disappeared!
- You decide to apologize to your friend, but before you can, you find out she's been telling lies about you — and you get mad all over again.
- Not only has the school fallen down, but you are trapped in the same room with your teacher and he's badly hurt.
- The pencil idea does seem bad enough at the moment, so maybe

we'd better just leave this one alone for now.

- There's definitely someone — or some*thing* — in the kitchen!

You've got your problem all set, and getting worse by the minute. Now it's time to stop writing and start thinking again. What are you going to do with this? Does it turn out funny, bad or sad? What do you want to happen, and how are you going to make it happen?

Don't worry if you don't know all the answers right now. You'd be surprised at how many writers don't know how their stories are going to turn out. There have been lots of times when I've said to myself after writing all morning, "How interesting. I didn't know that was going to happen!"

You might want to walk around and think about your story for a while at this point, or just sit and stare out the window. (My family still doesn't quite believe me when they walk into my room and find me sitting comfortably in a chair with my eyes closed and I tell them I'm *working*.)

You might even want to sleep on it again. When you do start getting it clear in your mind, it's time to face that paper once more and start jotting your thoughts down, even if it's only in point form.

Be sure you write them down, though. Don't count on remembering them later. I know from bitter experience that you probably won't. After having forgotten several ideas that I'm sure were absolutely, totally wonderful, I now keep a pencil and notebook with me all the time — even beside my bed at night.

Just the act of writing down all the ideas you've had so far will help you think of new ones and help you start to get your story in order.

That brings us back to something I mentioned in the first chapter: outlines.

Think of a skeleton,
not a cage

3

Outlines: sometimes you need them, sometimes you don't. Sometimes an idea for a story will come to you so complete and finished that all you have to do is sit there and try to write fast enough to keep up with it. That has happened to me, but only once or twice. Usually I have to organize my story before I start writing it. That's when I need to make an outline.

Start by jotting down on a clean piece of paper the original idea that you've now settled on, the problem that you invented and the complications you've already dreamed up. Then write down what you think will happen and how it will end (if you know).

Now expand on it as much as possible. How do the characters in your story feel about what's happening? Put that down. What do they do about it? Put that down. What happens in the end (if you know by now)? Get it all down.

As an example, let me go back to my three-legged-dog story and show you how my outline for that developed. First I started with just the bare details.

- Boy owns a valuable pedigreed golden retriever. (Original idea.)
- Dog loses leg. (Problem.)
- Boy wanted dog to be a show dog. (Complication.)
- Ending ?????????

Next I expanded on that in a second outline.

- Boy owns a valuable pedigreed golden retriever.
- Dog loses leg. (How? Possibly caught in a trap in the woods. Boy doesn't find it for days. How many days? Find out from vet how long a

dog must be in a trap to lose its leg but still be able to live.)

● Dog lives. Boy still loves dog, but is terribly disappointed that it will never be a champion now.

● Dog learns to get along on three legs better than most dogs could on five. Loves obedience training and is extremely good at it.

● Boy decides to enter dog in obedience trials and make it a champion that way.

Here I ran into a problem. Talking to the trainer at my own dog's obedience school, I found out that you can't enter a dog even in obedience trials unless it is "sound of limb." At that point my story seemed to have come to a dead end.

Then the trainer told me there were informal club obedience trials, the only difference being that the dog wouldn't become a recognized champion if he won them.

My immediate response was, "Oh,

this boy wouldn't want that for his dog. He wants the 'real thing.' "

Then my mind started working again, and here's how the outline went on:

- Boy finds out dog can't enter regular obedience trials.
- Trainer suggests boy enter dog in club trials because the dog is so well trained and loves the work so much.
- Boy rejects this angrily. That's not good enough for *his* dog.
- Trainer keeps insisting and finally, seeing how much fun the dog has doing obedience work, boy gives in and enters dog in club trials.
- Dog wins. (Is that it? Seems blah. Needs something more. Maybe it'll come to me as I write.)

Outlines are useful to get you going with your story, and also to show you where you might have to do some research before you actually start writing, as you can see from this example.

If, later on, your story suddenly

takes off and things start happening that you didn't know were going to happen — if the characters take over and start doing what *they* want to do instead of what you intended them to do — great! It'll mean your story is coming alive.

In that case, change your outline or expand it. It's not engraved in stone. An outline is meant to help you, not make things harder. Think of it as a skeleton that you can build on, not as a cage that hems you in and keeps you trapped.

* * *

With this dog story, by the time I'd finished the outline and started writing, I knew it would end with the dog winning, but I didn't know at that point *how* the dog would win. I just knew it was going to have to be something special.

When I got the boy to the club trials, which he still viewed with contempt, I was as surprised as he to find out that he was in fact as nervous as if the trials were "all for real."

The dog then took over my typewriter and just romped through those trials, having such a wonderful time that it won the whole thing. At the end, the judge announced that he had never awarded so many points to *any* other dog in *any* other show, formal or informal, before.

Then — I could see it as clearly as could be — the dog sat there in the winners' circle, balanced precariously on three legs, tongue lolling out of the widest laughing mouth possible on any breed of dog, and all the people around stood up and cheered.

The something special that I had needed had come to me while I wrote.

The outline had worked. It had pointed the way. After that, the story had just taken over and gone there.

Who's who
and which is what?

Main Characters.

4

You've got your outline. You've got at least a vague idea of what your story is going to be all about. But who is in it? Who is the main character? What is his or her name? What is he or she like? Who are the other characters? What are their names? What are they like? How old are all these people? How long have they known each other?

Start with the main character. You might want to make it your own self, or you might want to make it someone else. If you decide on someone else, then the first and most important thing is to find out the character's name.

Sometimes a name will just come to you. Sometimes you'll have to search for it. Once you've got it, write it down on a clean piece of paper. Then underneath write down everything you possibly can about this person.

It doesn't matter if you end up by using only some of this information in your story. The important thing is that you get to know this person as well as you know your own best friend — or better. When you do, you'll know how your hero or heroine will feel about the problems you've created, and possibly even how he or she will go about solving them.

Now do the same thing with every other person in your story (including the animals).

Quite often you'll find that while you're writing the story, somebody you didn't think was going to be important will gradually become more and more so.

This happened in one of my books. A girl who was going to be a minor character developed a very strong personality and finally became just as important as the two main characters. In fact, I had to keep her under control or she would have run away with the whole story! (Actually, I became so fond of her that I might just give her a book of her own one of these days.)

If you really get to know your characters as well as you possibly can, you'll find that they'll sometimes do their own talking. All you'll have to do is write the words down. If you try to make them say or do something that isn't right for them, they'll refuse!

I've often had times when things just wouldn't work out. And each time, after sitting back and taking a good look at what I was doing, I've realized that I was trying to make a person do or say something that was completely out of character.

I'd suddenly think, Jane (or Jim, or whoever) would never say that! She'd never do that! That's what the problem is!

I'd go back to my notes on Jane (or

Jim), start thinking once more about what kind of person she (or he) was, and try to figure out what the appropriate reaction *really* would be. Then I'd start writing again, and finally it would come out right.

Of course, if you decide to make your own self a character — perhaps even the main character — there's no need to write a sketch about yourself, is there? You know yourself, right?

Wrong! Just because you've decided to base a character on yourself doesn't mean that you have to tell the whole, complete, literal truth about yourself.

For the sake of your story you might want to change lots of things around. You could make yourself better than you really are, or worse. You could make yourself do all the wonderful things you wish you could, or say all the clever things you wish you had — or you could let yourself go and do something really nasty or bad that you would never dream of doing (or have the nerve to do) in real life.

You don't have to tell the truth. You can decide who's who and what's going to happen. You're writing the story and you're in control.

When my daughter was very young and I punished her once for lying, she said resentfully, "When I grow up, I'm going to be a writer and then I can lie all I want."

That's part of the fun of being a writer. In fact, you're *expected* to tell "lies." The truth is rarely interesting enough. You can change it around as much as you want in a story. You can change people, even yourself, to your heart's content.

But be careful if you decide to use yourself in a story. Something just might happen that I think I'd better warn you about. In the same way that you sometimes find out more about your characters while you're writing about them (even when you thought you knew them perfectly well before you started), you might also find out something more about *yourself* than you knew when you started. Rather scary idea, that, sometimes.

Another variation on this theme is to write in the first person (using "I," that is), but making it someone *other* than yourself.

You may actually be a girl named Mary, but decide to write a story from the point of view of a boy named Tom. Why not? It would be interesting to see if you could do it. If you are a boy, could you write from a girl's point of view? You might learn a lot from such an experience.

If you do a good job of getting to know your characters, the people who read your stories will feel that *they* have gotten to know your characters too. They'll believe in them and care about what happens to them.

When I finish a story, and even more so when I finish a long book, I often feel sad. I've come to know the young people in my stories so well that I don't want to say goodbye to them. I feel I'm going to miss them almost as much as I would miss my own children. In fact, in very many ways, the children in my books *are* my own children.

The characters you create will be your own children too, and your best friends. Even sometimes your enemies. The most important thing is that they will be real.

It's hard to dive
into cold water

5

Now let's get that story started. Again, nothing that you write is engraved in stone, so don't be afraid to put words down. You can always change them later. Just *get going*.

Think about the best books and stories you've ever read. Think about what made you choose those books or stories to read in the first place. Chances are it was the very first page or two. By the same token, you'll want your readers to be so interested by *your* first page that they'll just have to read on.

You'll also want to let your readers know as soon as you can *who* the story is about, *where* the story takes place, and *what* the problem or conflict is.

Introduce your main character, tell enough about him or her to let your readers know at least approximately how old he or she is, let your readers know where the setting is, and then bring on the problem.

Of course, you're not just going to say, "John Wigglestooth is nine years old and lives at 22 Maple Lane and his dog has just chewed up his mother's purse."

There's no drama in that, but there are lots of ways to get all the information in *while* you're getting your story going.

One way is to begin with *action!* Mom finding her chewed-up purse. The rotten kid pushing the cat into the toilet. The walls falling down around you and your teacher. A loud crash in the kitchen, or even just the doorbell ringing. How about:

I had to write a story by Monday, and here it was, Sunday night already. I was so nervous that I'd chewed my pencil until it looked as if a mouse had been at it. The eraser tasted disgusting, but I hardly even noticed it.

Suddenly, without warning, it came off in my mouth. At that very same moment, I hiccupped — and lodged it in my windpipe. I couldn't breathe!

Gasping for breath, I doubled over my desk. Air! I needed air before I choked to death. But I couldn't do anything. I needed help! Then the awful realization came over me that I was all alone in the house. There *was* nobody around to help!

Your readers know *who* the story is about (another kid, probably about the same age), *where* the story is taking place (in the main character's room at a desk), and you have certainly introduced the problem.

Another way is to begin with dialogue. Don't *tell* about the fight you and your best friend had; let whoever is reading your story *hear* it. Write it all down in quotes, as furious and bad-tempered and noisy as you can make it. For example:

"You *lied* about me, Sue Parker. To the whole school! You *lied!*"

"I did not! *That's* the lie and *you're* telling it!"

Sue had been my best friend for the past eight years — ever since kindergarten — and we'd never ever fought before. But she'd never ever lied about me before, either.

You've given your readers all the important facts in the first eight lines, and mainly through dialogue. You haven't even had to stop to identify the speakers, either, because the way you've written it makes it obvious who's who.

If you're going to write about the dog episode, how about starting with one loud scream . . .

"EEEEEEEEEEEEEK!!!!!!!!!!!!!!!!!"

The scream came from David's mother in the living room. At exactly the same time his brand-new pup flew into his room and scrambled under the bed, heading for the farthest corner. David had a horrible sinking feeling in the pit of his stomach.

"One more thing," his mother had said. "If that pup chews one more thing, he goes right back to the pound!"

The cat walked by, tail waving complacently. She looked smug.

Once in a while a flashback can be a good way to start off. I had a problem with one of my books. The story was about a young girl, Lady Jane Grey, who was Queen of England for nine days when she was only fifteen. But then the rightful queen, Mary, took her prisoner and ordered her head chopped off. (This is a true story, by the way. It happened in the year 1554.)

My problem was that the story had to start when Jane was nine years old, but most of the story takes place when she was older. I wanted people to know this. I didn't want to start with her being nine years old, or people would think the whole book was going to be about a nine-year-old girl, not a teenager. I solved the problem by the use of a flashback.

The story opens with sixteen-year-old Jane standing at the window of a house overlooking Tower Green, watching a scaffold being erected. She knows she is to be executed there that morning. Then I have her think back to how it all began.

She remembers the day when she was nine years old and the messenger came from London to tell them the news that her cousin Edward, exactly the same age as she, was now King of England, and that she was to go and live at court. The story picks up from there and then goes on until it gets back to the exact moment when it started.

Once, with another book, I had a terrible time with the first chapter. I wrote it and rewrote it and rewrote it and couldn't get it right. Finally I just gave up and went on with the story.

When I finished the book, I went back to rewrite the first chapter, and this time it worked. I guess I just had to get to know my characters a little better — and know what the book was all about a little better — before I could know how it should begin.

Take your idea and start experimenting with first paragraphs. Write two or three, or even more. Try several different ways until you find the way that seems to suit your story best.

The only way a story ever gets written is by starting it, so take a deep breath and dive in!

Stuck . . .

6

You're off to a great start, everything is going along fine, but suddenly the words stop coming. You know where you want to go — but how are you going to get there? What do you write next? You've ground to a halt. You're out of ideas. You're STUCK.

There's a name for this. It's called "writers' block," and it hits all of us sooner or later. I know, because I've wrestled with it many times. I sit down at the typewriter and just *can not* think of what I want to say next.

There are lots of ways to deal with this, however, so don't despair. Just consider yourself in the company of most of the writers in the world and learn a few tips from them.

The first thing to do is to *sit down at that desk!* If you walk around saying, "Oh, I just don't feel like writing today. I'll wait until I can think of something," that will be the end of your story. I've read dozens of articles by well-known and even very famous writers who say that the hardest part of writing is actually sitting down and getting to it. It's even harder when you know you're stuck.

I've been known to wash the kitchen floor in order to avoid my typewriter on some occasions, and if you were a member of my family you'd know how much I hate that particular chore. In fact, my son came home from school once, walked into the kitchen, and said, "Oh, oh, Mom must be stuck with her writing again. The kitchen floor's clean!"

Sitting down at that desk when it's the last thing in the world you want to do — when you're *afraid* to sit down at it — is called discipline. That's a word that's far more important to writers than the word "talent." You can be the most talented writer in the world, but without discipline you'll never get anything finished.

On the other hand, you may not consider that you have any talent for writing at all, but if you discipline yourself to try, you may surprise yourself and turn out something really good.

Once you're sitting at that desk, what do you do? You could start brainstorming again. What if this happened . . . ? What if that happened . . . ?

David and his mother have just had a terrible fight. She's ordered him to take the dog back to the pound. You know you want him to keep that dog, but how are you going to make him do it?

Start scribbling down any idea that comes into your mind that might solve the problem. Just the *act* of writing will generate more ideas.

Another trick is to start moving your character around. Make him do something, even if you don't think it has anything to do with your story. I got stuck quite early on in my book about Lady Jane Grey. I'd written the first chapter, got Jane and her family to London, and was all set to write about the young King Edward's coronation. Then I stalled.

How was I going to get them to the coronation? What should they do next? I sat and stared at the blank piece of paper with "CHAPTER 2" written on it and bit my fingernails. That wasn't very productive, and it certainly wasn't good for my fingernails.

So I bustled Jane's nurse into the room without the slightest idea of what she was going to do — and suddenly thought of clothes. Of course! Jane and her sister Katherine would have to have something to wear for the coronation.

The nurse immediately whisked over to a trunk, opened it, and took out Jane's and Katherine's best dresses, which they hadn't worn for a year. Then, of course, Jane's dress would be too small for her, so that would create a problem. Then, of course, Jane would be dejected

7

Almost as hard as starting — sometimes even harder — is knowing how and when to stop. With my Lady Jane book it was pretty obvious where the book was going to end. It was to go full circle, right back around to the beginning. Getting there, however, proved to be more difficult than I'd anticipated.

Towards the end, every day when my daughter came home from school she would ask, "Did you finish it today, Mom?" and I would have to answer, "Well, no, not quite yet. It's going to be a little longer than I thought."

Finally one day she said, "You know what the problem is, Mom? You just don't want to kill her off."

She was right.

Endings may be sad or happy, but they must make sense and they must satisfy your readers. You want people to love reading your story, to be sorry to finish it and to feel that the ending was just right.

You have to make sure that your main character has solved the problems (and don't let anyone else do it for him or for her), that she or he has solved them in a logical way, and that there aren't any loose ends left lying around.

By the end of a good story, your main character will have changed in some way. He or she won't be the same person as in the beginning. The character will have grown up a bit, or learned something, or done something that's affected his or her life.

The main player in your drama will have been actively involved instead of just sitting by and watching things happen.

Maybe the boy with the pup spends

every cent he's been saving for a bike on an obedience course for his dog.

By giving your friend a chance to explain — by trusting her — you discover the truth behind your argument.

By the time your hero at last finds that rotten kid, he's learned a big lesson about responsibility. (He's also learned how to get angry, wet cats out of toilets.)

You've got a great idea for the ending of the pencil eraser story. You could have the heroine — yourself or someone else — suddenly remember a TV show that she's seen, or a first-aid demonstration at school. She throws herself, stomach down, over a chair in her room as hard as she can and the eraser pops out. (This is beginning to sound more like a comedy!)

Your heroine has managed to save herself, and she's learned something in the bargain, if only not to chew on pencils — at least, not on pencils with erasers. (When you're doing your research for this one, you'd better check with someone who would know to see if all this is actually possible. If not, maybe this is the idea that ends up in the waste-basket.)

It's always fun to have a surprise ending after building up suspense all through a story. Let's get back to that noise in the kitchen.

You've decided to make your main character a boy named Tom, and you're going to write in the first person. It's almost dark and Tom is all alone in the house. He can't remember for sure if he even closed the back door, let alone locked it. There have been several bur-glaries in the neighbourhood.

There's another crash in the kitchen! Does he run? Does he try to get to the phone and call the police? Does he drag up enough courage to go and look? Let's say he does:

I took a deep breath.

"Don't be such a coward, Tom," I told myself, but I couldn't manage to convince my knees to stop shaking. I took another breath, then I opened the kitchen door.

The first thing I saw was a mess of broken dishes on the floor. The next thing I saw was a raccoon on the kitchen counter with his head in the cat-food bag. The cat was sitting on the counter right beside it, washing her face.

The back door *was* open, and Cleo had invited a friend in for supper.

We'd better not forget your teacher, stuck there with all those walls falling down around him. *Of course* you rescue him — at great risk to your own life and limb. And *of course*, as soon as he's well enough to come back to school he expects that story to be handed in.

What about the doorbell, I can hear you asking. Well, it's been ringing and ringing, and you are so busy with something really important that you just can't stop and go to answer it. Nobody else seems to be going either, however, so finally, with a huge sigh of exasperation, you go.

It's the mailman. Bringing you a registered letter with a cheque in it from a magazine that has just bought your very first story!

The trouble with titles

8

Unfortunately, books and stories have to have titles. I find making them up hard — sometimes almost impossible. When I start on a new story I rarely know what the title is going to be. Because I'm a fairly neat and orderly person, however, I like to see a title on the first page, so I stick something up there and call it my "working title." In the course of writing the story it usually changes several times.

The trouble with titles is that they have to do so many things. First of all, they have to tell people what the book or story is all about, or at least give a hint. But, at the same time, they can't be boring.

They have to be catchy or interesting. They can't be corny, they can't be dumb, they can't be drippy. The author, too, has to be comfortable with them. A title that has great meaning for the author, however, may mean nothing at all to someone else. It's no wonder that I'm not alone among authors in often putting off the naming of my books and stories until the very end. I found naming my children easier!

My first book was called *A Year for Growing*. The story was about a boy named Robbie who had to spend a year with his grandfather, and they didn't get on at all well. During that year they both changed and did a lot of growing. I didn't think of that title until I'd finished two drafts of the book.

Then, when the book was reprinted, the publisher decided it needed something snappier. It took me weeks. Finally, when I was doing a reading from the book to a school class, it suddenly hit me that Robbie felt that everything he did at first in this new and strange environment was wrong.

Out of the clear blue sky (or the well-lit classroom) the title *Wrong Again, Robbie* just jumped out at me, and that's what it is now called. The publisher was right, because when I ask, most kids prefer the second title. I even had one boy come up to me once and tell me that he'd bought the book because his name was Robbie and he was always wrong, too.

When I wrote a ghost story, my working title was *The Summer the Dolphins Came,* and I still like it best, although I can see that it wasn't too informative. There had to be something in the title to let people know it was a ghost story, so it became *The Haunting at Cliff House.*

Perhaps the easiest time I ever had with a title, and the only time that the title I started with stuck with the book all the way through, was when I wrote *The Other Elizabeth.* The story's about a girl named Elizabeth who goes back through time and takes the place of another girl named Elizabeth.

That one was easy. The one that came after wasn't so bad, either. In that book, another girl finds in a meadow a mysterious stone that also has the power to transport her back in time. The title was simply *The Stone in the Meadow*, although it did take me a while to think of it.

The next book was a killer. I'm not quite sure how many titles I went through on it, each worse than the last. I remember only one of them, *Journey into Tomorrow*, and that's so bad I have no wish to look back in my records to find out what the others were.

It wasn't until I was well on into the book that I stumbled on the right title. Rachel, the heroine, is very unhappy. She's made the unicorn the symbol in her own mind of all that is perfect and beautiful in the world, but, just as unicorns don't really exist, so she feels perfection and beauty will never really exist for her, either.

At one point she says, "I wish there *were* unicorns." As soon as she said it I knew that had to be the title of the book.

My story about the three-legged dog didn't get its title until I typed the very last words. At the end, when Jeff sees his dog sitting there so proudly in the winners' circle, and people are standing up and cheering, he realizes that his dog is a champion after all, just *A Different Kind of Champion.*

There are some tricks you can do to make your titles interesting. Alliteration is one — words that start with the same sound, whether or not they start with the same letter. *Wrong Again, Robbie* is an example of that; so is the title of this chapter.

Or you could make your title a question. I did that in a short story about a girl who was faced with a choice of which way she was going to go to school on a morning when she was already late. The whole of the rest of her life depended on the choice that she would make. I called that story *Which Way?*

You could make your title so unusual that it's intriguing. I called one short story *Coffee, Snacks, Worms.* I like to think nobody would be able to resist reading that one, if only to find out what the title means. Make the title contradictory. *To Last, You Have to Be First,* for example. Why not try a line of dialogue? *"I Hate You, Sue Parker!"* might make a good title.

One day a few months ago, I was struggling to think of a title for a small book I was writing for young people on how to write.

The day started out with me calling up to my son for the third time, "Chris! You're going to be late for school. Get out of bed right now!"

During the rest of the day I worked on my book.

After school it was my son's job to walk the dog. (Yes, still the same dog.)

"Chris," I reminded him, "don't forget to walk the dog."

"Later, Mom," he answered.

"No, not later. Right now!" I growled.

By dinnertime I hadn't yet come up with a title for that book. I called Chris to dinner.

"Be there in a minute," was the answer.

"Dinner's ready right now!" I shouted back.

Then something struck me. How many times a day do kids hear those words, "right now?"

And here I am right now, trying to write a book telling kids how to write . . .

How about . . . ?

For a title . . . ?

WRITE NOW!

Revision,
it's not a dirty word

9

The first drafts ~~of my manuscripts~~
My first

usually look ~~like this.~~ ~~Very~~
like this.   Messy

~~messy.~~ So messy, that probably no
in fact,

one except me could ever read
them.

That's fine. Because first drafts are for
your eyes only. The main objective is to
get your story down on paper — beginning, middle and end. I don't think I've
ever started a story or a book without a
dreadful, panicky feeling that I'm not
going to be able to finish it.

In fact, I usually stay fairly panicky
right up until the end. Only then, when
I've typed in the very last period, can I
relax and heave a sigh of relief. My story

is down on paper! It's rough, it's sketchy, it still needs a lot of work, but it's *down* there. The hard work is over. Now I can start to play.

It may sound strange to you to hear someone speak of revision as play, but in a lot of ways it really is.

You can look at your story carefully and see where it needs improvement. Perhaps you should explain something a little better. Perhaps you've spent too long describing something else and have interrupted your story. Perhaps the dialogue in one part sounds stilted.

Now's the time to go over everything and polish that story until it's absolutely the best that you can do at this time.

Have you ever stopped to think about what the word revision means? It is, literally, re-vision — seeing something again. That's what you will be doing now: looking at your story carefully for the second time and seeing what needs to be done to it.

Without the worry of "how is it going

to end?" and "how am I ever going to get this written?", it really is a time to enjoy.

There are limits of course. I wrote my first book several years ago. I sent it out to a publisher; the publisher sent it back. I sent it out again, and again the big, brown, bulky envelope came back. I decided that maybe I'd better reread it. It was now almost a year since I'd written it.

I reread it, and to my horror found that it wasn't nearly as good as I'd thought. So I sat down and rewrote it. (We're talking about a full-length book here. That's a lot of work.) Sure now that it was good enough to be published, I sent it out. Back it came.

To cut short the pain of remembering, I'll tell you that over the next six years I sent that manuscript out six times — and six times it came back. I rewrote it entirely three times, and bits and pieces of it I don't know how many times. It was getting pretty discouraging, especially since I'd written four more novels in those six years, and they were coming back too!

Finally, I sent it out one more time. When the mailman brought that disgustingly familiar brown package back yet again, I couldn't even bear to look at it. It lay on the hall table all day while I went around feeling very sorry for myself. It wasn't until late afternoon that I opened it. Sure enough, there was my manuscript — but this time an editor had written me a letter.

"Your manuscript is *almost* good enough to be published," he said, "but it needs a bit more work."

MORE WORK?

He then proceeded, for three single-spaced, typewritten pages, to make suggestions.

My first reaction was that if I had to rewrite that manuscript again, I'd be sick. My second reaction was that if an editor had bothered to take the time to write me such a helpful letter, it would be pretty dumb of me not to give it one more go.

Then I started thinking seriously about his suggestions and in spite of myself found I was getting enthusiastic all over again. Suddenly I couldn't wait to get going at it.

Dinner was late that night.

"You write well about animals," he had said. "Why not put in more about them?"

Robbie's grandfather had a wonderful hunting dog. What if Robbie turned up with a cat?

"Put in something about Robbie's school," the editor had said.

I didn't know exactly what I was going to do about that, so I just walked Robbie up to the front door of the school and decided to see what would happen. What happened was that two boys suddenly appeared (one of them called King-Size because he was so short) and they immediately became Robbie's very good friends — and major characters in the story.

How could I ever have left them out in the first place? When I'd finished rewriting the manuscript this time, it was a much better book — and the publisher accepted it.

When you've finished your second draft (or third, or fourth . . .) and you feel confident that you've revised your story to the best of your ability, then you have to tidy it up. This is the time to get out the dictionary, grammar book and thesaurus.

Check your spelling. Make sure every comma is in the right place and that your grammar would earn you an A in English class.

Have you used the same word several times? Unless you've done it on purpose and for a good reason, that's boring and bad style. Look it up in your thesaurus and find some synonyms to lighten and brighten up your prose.

It's time to make the final copy.

You've really worked on that story. It deserves the very best presentation you can give it. Do it credit by making it *look* as good as it is.

Whether you use a typewriter, computer, pen or pencil, the final copy should be as near to perfect in appearance as possible — everything neatly set up; titles, page numbers and your name in their proper places; not a smudge or a crossed-out letter anywhere.

* * *

You've done it. You're finished. Now look at that manuscript in front of you and tell me you don't feel proud — it may not have been easy, nothing worthwhile ever is — but it wasn't all *that* hard, was it?

Where are the brakes
on this thing?